INVESTING FOR SMART KIDS ACTIVITY BOOK

75 Activities to Learn How to Earn, Save, Invest and Spend Money

Christian Lee

INDEX

Introduction

Welcome to Investing for Smart Kids Activity Book. I hope you enjoy these pages and put each activity into practice.

If you made it this far, it's because you're a very smart kid who knows very well the importance of learning to manage money in a mature and responsible way.

In this book you will find practical tips, activities and exercises that you can do alone and with your parents or the adults responsible for you, so that together you can learn new life skills.

Remember that learning to generate, spend, save, economize, and invest your money can be the key to achieve all your dreams and plans for the future. Therefore, everything you put into practice from now on will impact your future.

Go for it little pal!

Message to parents and/or responsible adults

Dear parents, aunts, uncles, grandparents and/or guardians, thank you for committing to the financial education of your children, a key tool to form responsible adults with greater potential to fulfill their dreams.

This will be the first step for your little ones to begin to walk the path of responsibility, effort and the pursuit of results to pursue a fulfilling and purposeful life.

This material, specially created for them, seeks to implement in children's lives daily practices and habits that will help them to be their best versions before you, their peers, environment, and society in general.

Their accompaniment, their participation in this learning process and their interaction with these lines will be key.

So, I hope you too will enjoy this book as much as your little ones!

1

What is financial education?

Let's start at the beginning. In this book you will learn about the various tools and knowledge that are part of financial education, practices that you will repeat throughout your life and it is better that you do it consciously, attentively and from knowledge.

If you generate and manage your money responsibly from now on, you will be guaranteeing your comfort, access to better opportunities and it will be much easier for you to achieve your plans.

So, now I ask you: **what practices are included in financial education?**

Analyze the images and complete the following table:

2

Financial education tools

The tools of financial education are, precisely, tools that you will use throughout your life, consciously and responsibly, so that when you are an adult you can achieve your plans.

It is about healthy financial habits, always keeping in mind that your economy belongs to you and that you must make informed and educated decisions.

What financial education tools do you know?

_____

_____

_____

_____

Analyze the images and complete the following table:

3

Identifies mischievous goblins

It turns out that there are mischievous elves that place products that we should know when to ask our parents and when not to ask them, since it is very important to forge behaviors and habits because, although now our parents are the ones who can buy us things, later we will be the ones who will have to know how to discern between what to buy and what not to buy.

Many times, there are products in the supermarket that although they look like a lot of fun, they are misleading. They are food products that do not nourish your body or do you good, but on the contrary. And many times those same products, in order to seem more attractive, promise a toy that is surely fragile and of poor quality. Do not pressure your parents to buy them for you, you will see that if they do, you will be getting a fiasco and you will regret having done it.

Name four mischievous sprites who used to seduce you at the supermarket that you will now say no to.

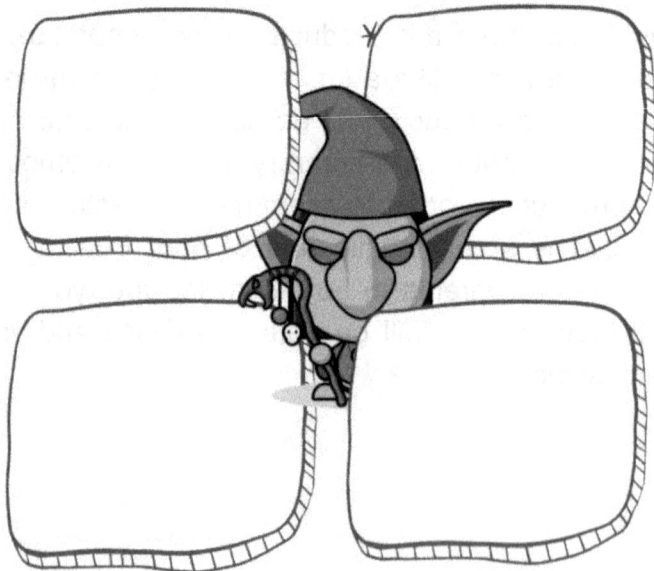

4

What is money?

In case you didn't know, your parents or the adults responsible for your upbringing must work to receive in return a sum of money that will serve to cover the expenses and needs of the home, the family, and of course, your own.

Money is represented in bills, coins, checks, or deposited in the bank and operating through debit cards, which serve as means to acquire goods. In other words, everything that is bought and sold is mediated by money.

Each country calls its currency differently and it is useful for the entire population to trade basic and luxury goods and services.

Do you know what your currency is? Draw a bill in the box below.

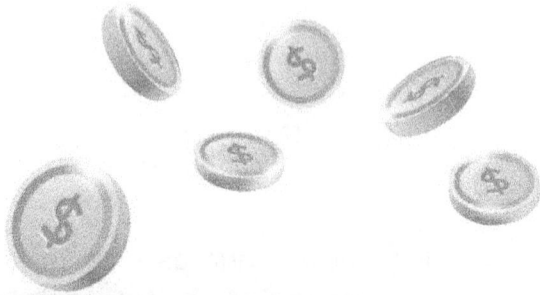

5

Goods and services you can purchase with money

You may not know it yet, but every time you visit the doctor, go to school, break in a new pair of sneakers or get a surprise toy, your parents must have paid for it.

In order to pay, your parents had to work very hard to get that money which they then put towards goods and services.

Goods are products that people buy either to eat, play, rest or facilitate some task. While services, which are not material things, generate convenience, well-being and comfort.

Complete in the following table four basic products and four basic services in your home by analyzing the images.

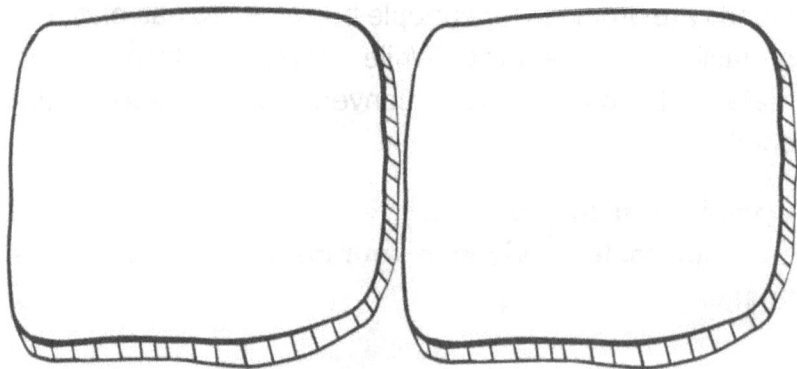

6

How is the money earned?

As I told you in the previous activity, to earn money you first must work. That is the only right way to do it.

Likewise, you can receive money by other means, but these will not be regular or long-lasting, so it is better not to get used to them.

One way to receive money other than by working may be because you received the proceeds of an investment, received a severance payment or inheritance, or won the lottery, for example.

Those ways I just named may happen to you from time to time, but it is not a recurring income, so it is better **not to count on them** for **your basic expenses.**

As an adult, in order to cover the basic expenses that your parents take care of today, you will have to work, economize, save, invest and know when, how and on what to spend.

How do your parents earn money?

_____

_____

_____

_____

7

What is your dream job?

Just as your parents have their jobs, when you grow up you will have yours too.

Keep in mind that working involves time and effort. As you may have seen, your parents must go to their jobs every day and do the tasks for which they are paid or for which they earn money.

In short, you get paid for your time and effort, meaning that the money will cost you those two things.

There are millions of jobs. Moreover, there are those with and without bosses. Your parents may work for a company, an institution or a business that does not belong to them, in which case they are employees, since there is someone who earns more and pays them for their services.

On the other hand, there are also those who are self-employed, i.e., they decided not to have bosses or a fixed salary, and they own their own businesses or companies or provide a professional service because they previously trained and studied.

Do you know what you want to be when you grow up?

_____

_____

_____

_____

Surely that's what you want to be is what will make you money.

8

Choose a profession

Precisely what you want to do and be when you grow up is what will give you the money to sustain your lifestyle, cover all your expenses and allow you access to indispensable goods and services as well as those that generate comfort and convenience.

Of course, the more you invest in the career you choose, the better professional you will be in it and therefore, the more money and recognition you will be able to earn.

The important thing to keep in mind is that whatever your dream job and the profession you want to dedicate your life to, it is key that you stay informed about it, train and educate yourself continuously.

If you want to be an astronaut and get paid for it, then take advantage of your free time to watch videos about the Universe and the advances in science, research NASA and its discoveries, pay close attention to your school classes and get used to the idea that you will have to go to college.

To manage your money well you must follow a concrete plan, have clear goals and future objectives that motivate you and work for you to delimit what is worthwhile and what is not.

So now I ask you to write down what your life goal is and three goals that will help you reach that goal.

9

Differentiating needs from wishes

Having clear and concrete future goals and objectives will guide you on your path to adulthood and you will be working on facilitating your access to money when you grow up. That's a good thing!

When you have clear goals and you actively work on them, it is much easier to know how to say NO to those things and situations that do not add or contribute anything to you.

While there are basic needs, such as eating, having a home, being able to access health and education, and receiving the attention and care of the adults responsible for your upbringing, there are desires that we may postpone or relegate because they may cost more than they are really worth.

What are the pillars and priority needs for your life?

_____

_____

What are the goods and services you could avoid?

_____

_____

_____

_____

10

Differences between what it costs and what it is worth

Many times, when we go to the supermarket with our parents, we ask them for things that we don't know how expensive they are, but many times they are not worth it. Now I will explain why.

A box of colorful cereal that includes a small toy, for example, and that you want very much but that perhaps the adults responsible for your upbringing tell you not to, costs much more than it is worth.

It turns out that a product that plays on TV, computers, tablets and cell phones funny videos for you to buy, is spending money on it and you are the one paying for it by buying this product.

So, in the supermarket, that box of cereal with toy not only costs the cereal and the toys, but also the video they showed you, and a whole marketing and advertising process that I will explain later.

Besides, they worked so hard to get that cereal box to you and sell it, that they forgot about the quality of the cereal. So, if you buy it, you will quickly get bored of the little toy that comes with it and besides, you will not be feeding yourself for the purpose of being strong and healthy, you will only be filling your stomach for a while with things that do not do good to your little growing body that needs good fuel.

A very good way to differentiate between what it costs and what it is worth is, for example, to measure it in time. That is, if an ice cream costs twelve dollars, you can compare it in relation to how much work time it represents for your parents. To do this I suggest the following activity:

Ask your parents what their monthly salary is.

Dad:

_____

Mom:

_____

How many days and hours do you work per month?

Dad:

_____

Mom:

_____

Multiply the number of hours your parents work in a day by the number of days they work in a month.

Dad:

_____

Mom:

_____

Divide your parents' monthly salary by the number of hours they work in a month.

Dad:

_____

Mom:

_____

How much do your parents earn per hour of work?

Dad:

_____

Mom:

_____

11

Be clear about expenses

There is a very important issue of financial education that we will see right now. It is about income and expenses.

To lead a healthy financial life, it is very important that you learn to spend less than you earn, so that you have money to spare and not to lack.

Now that you know what the basic expenses are and what your parents' salary is, you can consider the two most important things in your household and family finances.

Then, the task I will give you next is to **complete the table with income and expenses, placing the basic needs, the costs in money and time of them**.

INCOME

TOTAL

BASIC EXPENSES

TOTAL

EXPENSES FOR THINGS WE WANT BUT CAN WAIT

TOTAL

EXPENSES

TOTAL

12

Compare values

You have reached activity number twelve and I must tell you that you are a very intelligent, attentive child, capable of achieving anything you set your mind to, because you learn very quickly and you know how to put into practice everything you assimilate. Well done! You will become a fulfilled and happy adult and you will achieve all your goals and objectives!

You know:

- what is financial education?
- what it is used for
- what is money?
- how to get it?
- what you can buy and pay with it
- you know how to differentiate between basic and necessary expenses and those that are only desires
- you understand the difference between what it costs and what it is worth.

And there is still a lot to learn!

Now I want to talk to you about something I already told you in a previous activity, about the cost and value of each thing we need or want.

The best way for you to size up the costs of things, whether they are goods or services, is to compare.

How much does a soft drink cost at the club?

_____

How much does the same soft drink cost in the supermarket?

_____

How much would you save if you bought it at the supermarket?

_____

13

Desire or necessity?

We come to a key issue for children, who if they learn to recognize this important difference now, will be much more intelligent and successful adults than most of today's elders.

I have already advanced you some things in relation to this topic, but I would like to go a little deeper.

It is very well that from time to time you satisfy some desire you have, the important thing is that this is not repeated too often and becomes a daily habit.

It is not the same if you eat french fries on the weekend than if you order them every day. Or playing four hours of video games a day to playing only on Sundays. It's about finding the balance between what you want, always prioritizing what you need.

You must train yourself and learn to master your impulses and emotions to make decisions from reason and not from desire. Always seeking to maintain in time those actions that enrich you and reducing those that take away your energy without giving you anything more than instant fun.

If you are thirsty, you may want a soft drink, but what you need is water. Does this mean you should never drink a soft drink again? NO, of course not. Just that for a week, a month and a year, you should have drank more water than soda, read more books than played video games, brushed your teeth more days than not, and so on. That's what habits are all about.

So, when it comes to managing your money, you might think: if you're saving up to buy a new toy and you get thirsty, maybe you'd be better off carrying your water bottle instead of buying a drink. Because you have to understand that you can't have it all. You have to learn to choose.

Needs are indispensable. Wishes are not, therefore, not all desires will be fulfilled, only those that you consider most important and that will make you the happiest one.

Circle what you need to resolve each emotion.

Hunger: food - snacks - soft drinks - sweets - potato chips

Boredom: reading - going to the park - buying a new toy - buying a new game for play station

Thirsty: water - soft drink - ice cream - get angry

Sadness: hug your parents - tell your parents what is happening to you - write down your emotions in a notebook

- talk to a sibling, cousin or friend - throw a tantrum - ask
for things

14

Recognize your mood before spending money

Many times we may feel sad and frustrated, either because our parents did not give us the attention we needed, because our friends made fun of us or because we got a bad grade in school.

When we feel like this, with low energy and strength, it is very common that we think that buying something will make us feel better. Then we pressure our parents to buy us that toy or that candy and we throw tantrums.

That is not a mature or intelligent attitude, because it will not lead you to solve anything of what happened to you or what is happening to you. On the contrary, what it will generate is that what is hurting you is repeated and becomes a habit.

Therefore, you must recognize your emotions and communicate them. If your parents didn't pay attention to you today, it's probably because they came home tired from work or because they didn't have a good day, talk to them, let them know how you feel.

Things won't be solved with a new toy or a treat. They will be solved if you take action and communicate to adults what is going on with you, the problems you are having and the difficulties you are facing.

Ask for a meeting with your whole family. Tell them that from now on you need half an hour a day to meet and talk. In that half hour it is important that the whole family be in a place in the house where they can relax and talk about how each one's day went.

What time will it be?

15

Beware of Misleading Marketing and Advertising

I already told you a bit about this a few pages earlier, but now we will go deeper into the two concepts.

It turns out that there are billions of products in the world that we can buy and so they compete with each other.

We find hundreds of choices at the toy store, the supermarket or the mall. But we are more likely to choose those brands that appear on our mobile devices, tablets, computers and televisions. Or on the billboards we see on the streets.

I already told you that this is not strategic because placing a sign on the street or sending you a video costs money, money that is included in the price of that product, therefore, making it more expensive.

Marketing and advertising is just that, a way to sell by generating in you the need to buy what they offer you.

So, you go down the street and you see a sign that says that with these shoes you will run like a champion, and the truth is that this is not true. To run like a champion you have to train, not buy the most expensive shoes.

Therefore, you must be very attentive in life and not allow yourself to be deceived by these things.

What makes you more fun?

_____

How can you run faster?

_____

What foods nourish you?

_____

Which drink quenches your thirst?

_____

How can you be top of the class?

_____

16

Manage your own money

Now yes, dear friend, we can say that you are ready to manage your own money. Let's go for it!

It is time for you to tell your parents everything you have learned so far and ask them to give you the confidence to manage your own money.

The proposal you will take to your parents is the following: ask them to convert the daily money they give you to spend at school or at the club into a weekly amount, and give it to you every Monday.

This way you can manage your daily consumption and decide what to do with your money every day.

How much is your allowance?

17

Increase your income

As you know, to increase your income you must work, but since you are a child and have your own chores and responsibilities as a child, you cannot go out and look for a job now.

So, what I propose to you is to offer different services to your parents. For that, you need to know their needs.

For example, at home, someone must maintain order; clean the furniture and floors; clean the kitchen and bathroom; make the beds; wash the car; wash, dry and fold the clothes; wash and store the vegetables and fruits in the refrigerator; wash, dry and store the dishes; walk the dog and clean its poo; clean the garden and pool.

As you will see, there are many activities at home that, in addition to working outside the home, your parents are responsible for. You can collaborate in these tasks in exchange of a small salary.

What services will you offer your parents?

18

Multiply your money

Way to go little pal, you're doing great!

Not only do you know about financial education tools, but you already have your own money. Well done!

Now comes a key concept to make your money multiply without too much effort. I'll tell you how.

Investing is a process by which using the money you have, you transform that capital into a larger sum. A clear example of investment is studying. Being able to study implies money. You have to pay for school, uniforms, school supplies, transportation, among other things. But all that money that is invested in studying is used so that in the future you can earn money in a more comfortable and practical way.

Because when you are an adult, if you don't have a profession or don't know how to do anything, it will be very difficult for you to get a job that pays you enough money to live comfortably. On the other hand, if you are a professional and offer a service that you guarantee to do well, people will pay you what you ask for.

An investment promises that what you spend now will be multiplied in the future.

Right now it is your parents who are investing in your education, since they are the ones who put up the money, but you are the one who puts in the time. Therefore, an investment of time that you must make and it is your obligation and responsibility is to study.

Now, I guess what you are looking for is an idea to multiply your money, the money you earn from your allowance and your salary. So, here are a few ideas:

You can buy the necessary ingredients to make cookies, chocolates or lemonade and sell them on weekends to your colleagues, neighbors, friends and family.

Also, you can select all those toys and clothes that you no longer like, don't fit or are not for you and with your parents' permission have a garage sale. In this case you will not be the one who invested in those products that you are going to sell, so it is very important to ask the adults responsible for you if you can get rid of those things.

What are you going to sell?

How much did you spend on the products you will sell?

Adding the value of your time, how much will each product cost?

19

Save

You already have an allowance, a salary and an investment. Now, saving is the key.

It is not only about generating money, but also about knowing how to spend it, how to invest it and how to save it.

The best way to save is to have a specific amount to set aside for savings, an idea of what you want to buy or invest with that money, and a transparent jar to keep your coins and bills in so you can keep track of your progress.

Find a clear glass jar and place your first savings in it. Then, mark the weekly evolution here.

20

Compound interest

Now you are a hard-working, responsible child who is focused on your goals and objectives, but when you are older and have your bank account, you will also be increasing your income simply by having your money in the bank.

So that you can begin to familiarize yourself with this tool that will undoubtedly encourage your savings, you could propose to your parents that for every ten dollars of savings they give you one dollar as a reward for your ability and behavior.

In adult life it is a percentage that the bank gives you for having your money stored there, the more money you have, the more money it will give you. This way you will be multiplying your money in a passive way that does not take up your time.

Then, propose to your parents that they reward your ability to save by giving you extra money for each savings figure you achieve.

21

What does it mean to have capital?

Let's review:

- you already have your allowance
- you have your salary
- you receive a return on an investment
- you have savings
- Some people reward your savings by giving you an extra amount for each figure you increase.

All these are your incomes. At the same time, you also have outgoings, such as:

- expenses on recreational activities
- an outing with friends
- a toy you want to buy
- a gift for mom and dad
- the money you invest in purchasing the ingredients of the product you sell and that gives you profit.

That money you spend buying the ingredients for your cookies or your lemonade that you will later sell, is your capital. Capital is money destined to generate more money, that is, to generate a profit.

Every time you sell a cookie you are earning, that is, you are profiting.

It is important that the money you capitalize, that is, that you use for an investment, such as buying the ingredients for the cookies, is reproduced, because otherwise instead of winning you will be losing.

Then, it is better to keep it separate, you can have a jar called "capital cookies", and in it put the amount needed to buy all the ingredients. That jar should always have that capital.

When you make the cookies write down how much you spent, then when you have sold them all write down how much you earned. Subtract from that value what you spent, what is left over is your profit. What you get back will be your capital again.

How much did you spend on the ingredients for your cookies?

_____

How many cookies came out with all these ingredients?

_____

Divide the total spent by the total number of cookies.

The result is the cost of each cookie, to which you must add your labor, i.e. your work (the value of your time), how much will each cookie cost?

22

Your word is a contract

Whenever you make a proposal and commit to do something, you must deliver. That is not negotiable. If you don't deliver, your word loses value and no one will bet on you again.

The most important thing you have is your word and when you make a deal, whether it is spoken or even better if it is in writing, that is very valuable and you must respect it.

If you proposed to your parents to receive a weekly allowance, which you will manage, remember to follow through. That means, if you spend all your money for the week on Monday, you can't go around on Tuesday complaining and asking them for more money to take to school. You gave your word and they have an agreement.

Also, if you agreed to walk the dog and pick up its poo in exchange for pay, do the job responsibly and follow through with the proposal you made in order to demand your pay.

And it's no good getting angry if your parents don't give you that extra tip for saving a certain amount of money if you don't make up that amount, because if you didn't, you don't deserve it.

The same is true for cookies. You are responsible for the capital to make them as well as for making and selling them. You made a commitment to do so. So make them yourself, leave the kitchen as you found it and spend your own money to buy the ingredients. Don't use the ones in the house and don't leave everything dirty and untidy.

In this way people will not only believe in you but will bet on you and all your capabilities. Having others trust you is the key to progress and achieve your goals, because you will always need the contribution of others.

So now, find the contract you need in the index of this book, fill it out and sign it between you and your parents or the adults responsible for your upbringing.

23

Expenditure/Investment

As you may already know, there are several types of expenses. They all vary according to the functionality and impact they have on our lives.

An expense that means an investment is, for example, paying for your school, buying your uniform and school supplies, paying for your transportation. Thanks to that you will be a great professional when you are an adult.

In order for you to be able to study, your parents invest money that they get by giving their time and you invest time that you put into studying and preparing yourself.

Write down here the investments of time and money you are currently making:

_____

_____

_____

_____

24

Expense/Savings

Another expense that will always be present in our lives is savings.

Now that you're a kid, if you want a new toy, to go out with friends or buy a bike, you can save up for it.

When you are an adult and want to buy a house, a car, a cell phone or invest in a business, you will need to save for it.

But there are also ways to save money that are not specifically by keeping money in a jar, but by opting for more economical products.

For example, if instead of buying a piece of candy every day at the school store, you buy a pack of candy at the supermarket and put one a day in your lunch box, you will be saving money.

If instead of buying a pair of sneakers from the brand that is the most fashionable and most publicized, you choose a lesser-known brand, you may even be able to buy three pairs Instead of one for the same amount of money.

If you take care of electrical energy by turning off the lights in spaces where no one is present and unplugging appliances that are not in use, you will be helping your parents to save on the electricity bill, and that would mean that they will have more money available for the family.

These are excellent savings techniques.

What will you do to save from now on?

_____

_____

_____

_____

25

Expenditure/Need

Another important expense that will be maintained throughout your life are the fixed expenses to cover basic needs.

Food, rent or mortgage payments, housekeeping, personal hygiene, health, education, taxes and utilities are very necessary to ensure a good quality of life and survival. You cannot eliminate them from your plans and should always be able to cover them.

Mark with a cross which basic expenses are necessary for life and which can be postponed.

Food

Latest model of running shoes

Personal hygiene

Household cleaning

Four-story hamburger patty topped with cheddar cheese

Rent or mortgage

Taxes

Services

Bank

Credit card

Education

Physical activity

Family leisure

Travel to Disney World

26

Expense/Expense

Lastly, and the only expense that can be postponed or suspended, is the expense destined to enjoyment, i.e., relaxation and fun.

There are many ways to have fun and relax without spending money, such as going for a walk in the park, riding a bike or playing with the family.

Therefore, it is very important that above all, in order to enjoy yourself, you learn to value time more than money. Because in order to relax, what we do need is time and many times, because of overspending we are worried or we add more work to be able to pay for everything we buy.

It is important that you learn to choose very well what you want to spend your time and money on so that fun, relaxation and enjoyment are real.

Write down five ways to enjoy, relax and have fun without money and five with money.

With money:

No money:

_____
_____
_____
_____
_____

27

Decide what to spend your time on

We are almost halfway through the activities in this book, and I assume that by now you understand the relationship between time and money.

To get money you invest your time. That's what you do when you work, you invest, you look for cheaper prices to save and you plan a life with goals and objectives.

That's why your time is the most valuable thing you have. Your time is the first product/service you have to offer, so the more things you can do in an hour, for example, the more your time will cost.

Someone who only knows how to sweep for one hour will not charge the same as a person who can do calculations and can get five results in that period of time. The second person for that same hour of time will produce more money.

For this reason, there are times that cost more than others.

The way you make your time more expensive is by adding value to it. You add value to your time the more you know how to do things that are led to what you want to do in the future.

For example: if you want to be a business administrator when you grow up, you can start right now to put into practice all the activities in this book, save, invest, economize, and add value to your time in this area. It won't do you any good to know how to play the piano or be a great draftsman. Therefore, there are many things that you will be discarding in your life and that's okay, because you are following a path.

First set a big goal, the dream of your life. Then set goals, which will be steps to follow to achieve that goal. Make a plan of action in which every day you must do something to accomplish a goal and get closer to your objective. Have a strategy.

I leave you a blank sheet of paper to write your action plan, that is, your strategy to meet your goals and achieve your objective.

My action plan

_____

_____

_____

_____

_____

_____

_____

_____

28

Decide what to spend your money on

Just as you are responsible for choosing what to do with your time, so it is with money.

It's about using money wisely so that it makes easier to get the achievements you want to accomplish in your life.

Write down four uses of money. I'll leave you with the first one:

To guarantee a home with all the comforts.

_____

_____

_____

_____

29

The added value

I already told you a little about what added value is, a way in which the same product or service makes a difference and stands out from others.

As you know, there are millions of competing products, thousands of brands selling the same thing but looking to make a difference and reach more customers or buyers.

I will give you an example that can help you in your daily life. Let's suppose you have an exam, answering all the questions correctly already guarantees you an excellent grade, but surely other colleagues will also do it. Anyway, your added value in that exam, and what will make you stand out, can be your writing style or your neatness, clarity and order within the paper.

If you are selling cookies, you know that you are competing with many others. So, to win more customers you can think about the features that will make them buy your product and not another. They can be:

- Quality of ingredients
- Taste
- Aesthetic presentation
- Good price

- On-time delivery
- Free tasting

That free tasting will be an added value to your product that people will appreciate. Just like children's playrooms in restaurants, free samples or gifts included with the purchase of a product.

What added value can your cookie sale have?

_____

What added value can your home cleaning and tidying service provide?

_____

What added value can you offer as a student?

_____

30

Buy low and sell high

Most businesses we know buy products cheaper and then sell them more expensively. So the secret as a consumer is to skip some of the steps a product goes through.

I'll give you an example. The milk you have in your refrigerator traveled several places before it reached your table:

First, a farmer milked the cow, and let's suppose he sold it to a company that deals with pasteurizing milk and packaging it in bottles. The farmer sold a liter of milk for 0.20 cents.

The bottling company will sell the milk bottles to a wholesale market for 0.40 cents each.

Then, that wholesale market will sell the milk bottles to smaller supermarkets at 0.60 cents each, so that your parents can buy it at 0.80 cents.

As you can see in the example, the farmer, the packaging company, the wholesale market and the supermarket all add value to the product and generate a profit in the process.

You can do the same. For example, if you know of a delicious, in-demand, hard-to-find treat, if you buy it in bulk you can sell it for a higher price in smaller quantities.

Keep in mind that you will always find cheaper those products that come in larger quantities. For example, if you buy a kilogram of jelly beans for 4 euros and you divide it into ten packs of one hundred grams, you can sell these smaller packs at 0.80 cents each, you would be recovering your initial 4 euros and earning 4 euros more.

The next time your parents go to the store, go with them, and with your savings buy a big package of candy that you know your colleagues like. Then buy small bags to break them up and sell them. To define the price answer these questions:

How much did the package of candy cost?

How much did the bags cost to break up the candy?

How many bags of goodies did you manage to put together?

Divide your total expense by the number of bags of goodies you put together. The result is:

Add to the above result the value of your work time and that will be the price of each bag of goodies. The value is:

31

Personal income and expenses

Let's review your income or potential income:

- Counter
- Charging for domestic services (what we call in adult life a salary)
- Profits from your investments: sale of cookies, sales of fractional products at higher prices
- Savings reward (what in adult life is bank interest)

These are the sources of income that you have generated and that serve to pay and buy what you need and want.

The important thing to know how, when and where to spend is to have a record of income and expenses, which are your expenditures.

Always remember that your expenses should be less than your income, because if you try to spend more than you have, there will be things you won't be able to afford.

What are your expenses?

_____

_____

_____

_____

32

Define your financial goals and objectives

As you already know, there are basic, everyday expenses that are impossible to avoid, they make up our lifestyle.

On the other hand, there are expenses that have to do with our desires and much better if they are aligned with goals and objectives.

If instead of thinking of going to the amusement park as a recreational or leisure expense you replace it with going to a science museum, you are spending on leisure and investing in knowledge at the same time. Therefore, it means that you are saving time and money.

You need to know what you want to do with your money, as this will give you more motivation to work, save and invest.

Part of your savings may be earmarked to buy a new game, for example. So chase that goal until you achieve it and don't get distracted along the way.

What are your financial goals and objectives?

_____

_____

_____

_____

33

Making a plan

Dear friend, don't forget that finances are a plan, so you must know your economy all the time, to know what to spend and what to save for.

Just as we are talking about having goals and objectives to make dreams come true, you must have a financial plan to achieve what you set out to do.

If your goal is to be a renowned economist and give lectures around the world, you must first finish high school, college, graduate school, a master's degree, work on your ventures or in companies. Each of these steps will be a goal to reach your big goal.

Each goal has its own daily tasks that you must develop, and I assure you that all of them need one or both of these two things: time and money. And to have time and comfort to study you need a backing of money, as well as to have money you need to invest time.

Therefore, to make your investment of time and money effective, you need to have a plan. In your plan you will include basic expenses, investments, savings, what you will use those savings for and the tasks you have taken on.

I leave you a chart so that you can define all these questions.

ACTIVITIES THAT REQUIRE TIME

To study	
To Invest	
Service you offer	

ACTIVITIES THAT REQUIRE MONEY

Save money	
To Invest	
Entertainment consumption	

WHAT INVESTMENTS DO I MAKE

WHAT ARE MY SAVINGS FOR?

34

The time value of money

Money and time are closely linked.

You know that to get money you need to invest your time, that's what you do when you work.

You are also aware that the more tools, knowledge, experience and quality your service offers, the more expensive your time will be, therefore you will be able to earn more money in less time.

You know the benefits of putting money away and having the bank pay you for it. And this, remember, is a matter of time. Bank interest that is daily, weekly, monthly and yearly will accrue as your money stays in the account. Therefore, time will be rewarding you.

Another way to use time to your advantage in relation to money is when you lend it.

For example, if a colleague, friend, cousin or sibling wants to buy a certain candy or toy but has spent all his money and has to wait until next week but doesn't want to because he wants the product so badly, you can lend him money. If you do, you can ask for collateral and interest.

The guarantee can be something that is worth the same or more than the amount of money you are lending him, for example, if you lend him 5 euros, you can ask him for a toy, school supplies or something that guarantees that he will pay you back the following week. When he pays you back, you will give him that guarantee.

As for interest, interest increases in relation to time. If today you lend him 5 euros, in seven days he must pay you back 7 euros, in fourteen days 9 euros, and so on. You can choose the percentage you want.

How is a percentage calculated?

Take a number, divide it by 100 and then multiply it by the percentage you want.

If the interest rate is 2% and you borrow 5 euros, how much should you get back?

35

Smart shopping

In the previous activity I gave you the example of a child who wants a toy but has spent all his allowance and no longer has the money to buy it. Now I ask you, **is it smart to ask for 5 euros and return 7 euros to buy a toy?**

Well, the truth is that it is not, since it is not a basic or urgent need or expense. Besides, if he waits until next week when he will receive his allowance again, he will pay 5 euros for that toy instead of 7, since he will end up paying 2 euros more for that toy when he asks you for it.

That's what smart shopping is all about.

Name one non-essential product you would like to purchase:

Have you already covered your basic expenses, savings and investment money?

Do you have the money to buy it?

Can you get it cheaper at another store?

What will be your smart plan?

36

Benefit coupons

Benefit coupons exist in real life. In the adult world, you will often find various coupons for discounts or for products or services that you can access through points.

For example, if you always go to the same supermarket, the ticket can give you discount coupons that will generate savings on your next purchase.

Another example is the miles you earn as you travel by paying for tickets with the same credit card. These miles are then converted into points that you can exchange for tickets.

What you can do to enjoy these benefits and learn how to use them is to create your own coupons and take a proposal to your parents to fund them.

In this case, you will have to give all the coupons to your parents, since you are the one who will earn as you fulfill a responsibility and do an extra task.

These coupons can be exchanged for recreational and leisure activities and for financial support for what you want to buy.

Ask your parents if they are okay with you creating coupons, and if they say yes, look in the index of the book to see where the cut-out coupons are located.

37

Money cycle

Experiencing the cycle of money from the moment it enters your life until it leaves is very important to know its real value, since obtaining it costs time and effort.

Therefore, to reaffirm everything you have learned in this book, I invite you to complete the following boxes of the money cycle.

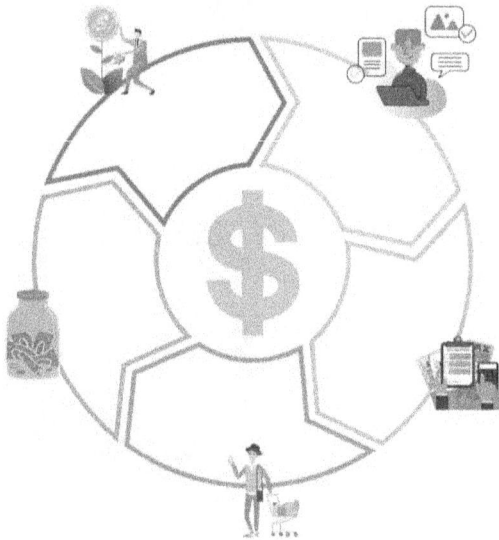

38

What can money buy and what can't?

As you have seen up to this point, money allows you to access services, products and facilities to meet goals and get closer to objectives. But there are some things that money cannot buy, such as love, family union, friendship, or talent. Those are things that can be in us and our environment despite the lack of money.

In addition, we are all capable of generating money if we set our minds to it and if we work with discipline, persistence, perseverance and willpower in pursuit of a plan.

No matter where you start from, the procedure to generate money is the same. But money is not going to guarantee everything that makes your life, there are things that are not bought or paid for with money and have to do with the quality of person you are.

Empathy, generosity, love, mutual help, understanding and forgiveness are necessary traits to enjoy a life with good friends and family, with whom you can enjoy and celebrate your achievements and your money.

Write down four things that can be bought with money and four things that cannot.

I can buy with money:

_____

_____

_____

_____

I can't buy with money:

_____

_____

_____

_____

39

What is economizing?

You are already putting it into practice:

- the administration of your allowance
- working for a "salary
- investing for profit
- save to earn interest
- lend to earn interest
- buy in bulk cheaper and sell in small packages more expensive
- use coupons to spend less
- not to choose the latest trends because they are more expensive due to higher marketing and advertising investment.

Precisely, these last two, which you have surely already marked as learned and put into practice, are related to economizing.

Economizing means reducing everything that takes time and money away from you, therefore, you can not only economize in your purchases, but also in your life in general.

When you define an economic and life plan you are economizing, because you eliminate many activities and things that you no longer need or that do not lead you to what you want to achieve.

There are thousands of ways to economize, for example:

Bathing efficiently, i.e., soaping your body, washing your hair, rinsing and getting out of the bath. No singing under the shower, playing or acting. You will be saving water, energy and time.

Keep only the things you need and sell or donate the rest. This way you save the time you spend cleaning and tidying your room.

Unplug appliances that are not in use and turn off lights in rooms where no one is present. This reduces energy consumption, which is very costly.

Make purchases for the home in quantity, since larger products are always cheaper than smaller ones.

Using public transportation instead of the car saves time and money, since the transportation ticket is cheaper than fuel.

And so there are many other ways to economize that you will become aware of throughout your life.

I recommend that the next time your parents go to the supermarket you accompany them, and make the following records:

How much does a kilogram of rice cost?

_____

How much does a five-kilogram package of rice cost?

_____

What is the price difference between the two?

_____

40

What is equity?

Wealth is everything you have. Everything material as well as the obligations and responsibilities that it implies.

For example, the house where you live (if it is not rented) is part of your parents' estate. In turn, the taxes and utilities they must pay on the house are also part of your parents' estate.

In the current society in which we live, our patrimony is something that no one can take away from us to give it to someone else, since it belongs to us by right.

Everything that has been given to you or that you have bought yourself, such as toys and clothes are your patrimony, and therefore, neither your classmates, friends, cousins or siblings can take them away from you, because that would be theft.

At the same time, your parents' estate will be yours and your siblings' if they inherit it. That is why it is important to take care of it.

Make a list of everything you own, transform each item into a price (its current market value) and add it up.

What is your net worth?

_____

What is your parents' net worth?

_____

41

What is a bank?

A bank is a company that is financed by shareholders' and customers' money.

Its service is to safeguard your money, generate interest and capitalize your investments.

It also offers products such as credit cards and loans.

None of the services and products offered are free, no matter how much it may seem so. Clients and investors must pay and provide guarantees, which, in case of non-payment, are appropriated by the bank.

That is why it is very important to be extremely responsible when accessing the bank's products and services, because if you don't pay, they can keep your things.

Which banks do you know?

_____

_____

_____

_____

What bank products and services do your parents use?

_____

_____

_____

_____

42

Accrued expenses

Ancillary expenses are expenses that go unnoticed because they are very small and common.

I don't know if it has ever happened to you to arrive at school and think that maybe you haven't loaded your notebook, but then you realize that you have. That happens because it's an everyday task that you do without thinking about it.

There are some expenses that are similar to that example. Maybe every morning when you get to school you buy the same candy. Maybe you haven't stopped to ask yourself if you really like it, if you want it, or if you really want to buy it.

It happens that you have become accustomed to doing it and it has become an automatic action. And maybe you think that buying it or not will not impact your savings, but I invite you to perform the following calculation:

How much does that daily treat you buy automatically cost?

Multiply its value by the five days of the week. How much do you spend weekly on that goody?

_____

How much is your weekly allowance?

_____

What percentage of your weekly allowance do you spend on that treat?

_____

How useful is it for your plan to buy it?

_____

Would you prefer to buy something else?

_____

An ant expense prevents you from making other expenses as it gradually takes away your money. Maybe, instead of buying that daily treat, once a week you can go out to lunch with your friends after school.

43

Selling and buying

Remember that we are often buyers and sometimes sellers.

In your case, every time you go to buy something you are a buyer. But when you offer a product or service you are a seller.

When you offer to clean your parents' living room for a tip, sell cookies to your family, sell fractional products to your friends or even lend money, you are a salesperson.

Being a buyer and being a seller have their responsibilities. As a buyer you buy less than you earn. As a seller you deliver what you offer.

That way, everyone wins and no one commits infractions.

Write four examples of buying and four examples of selling in the boxes below:

44

Financial skills

Everything we have been learning and putting into practice up to this point are financial skills that will impact your life experience from now on.

Keep in mind that the more skills you have, the more your time will be worthwhile and the easier it will be for you to achieve everything you set out to do.

All life skills can be learned and put into practice, and there are many different ones, such as:

- Interpretation and communication skills
- Emotional skills
- Problem solving and analysis skills
- Motor skills
- Financial skills

The better you are at communicating and understanding others; mastering your impulses and understanding your emotions; not hiding from problems but solving them; connecting with your body and executing the movements you propose; doing with your time and money what you really want for your life; the closer you will be to having a fulfilling life.

So, tell me what skills you think you have or want to develop from the ones I just mentioned:

_____

_____

_____

_____

45

Financial habits

A habit is something you do in a repetitive and automated way over a period of time. These are actions that, being familiar and common to us, soon become everyday.

Examples of habits are brushing our teeth as soon as we get up, getting dressed before going out, locking the door when we leave home. These are things we don't ask ourselves whether to do or not, whether they are right or wrong, we just do them.

Fortunately, we are able to eliminate, modify and create new habits. Of course, at the beginning it costs more, but as we repeat it, it becomes easier and easier.

You can create the habit of getting up early, making your bed, saving, studying a specific number of hours a day and so on.

All you need to do is pay attention to everything you want to do and do whatever you set your mind to, whether you feel like it or not, whether you are in the mood or not.

Remember that at the beginning it will be difficult, but later it will be very easy.

What financial habits do you want to have from now on?

_____

_____

_____

_____

46

Responsible consumer

Being a responsible consumer from now on will avoid many bad experiences that you may have as an adult.

As I told you a few pages ago, it is key that you spend less than you earn and that you are careful when accepting the products and services offered by the bank.

It turns out that many people, who do not know how to control their impulses or who want to have a lifestyle that they are not able to afford because they earn less than they spend, turn to loans and credit cards to pay for those ant expenses or expenses that are not basic but rather luxuries.

If you do not want to go through uncomfortable and frustrating situations because you do not have money to pay your bills, it is important that you work,economize, save, invest and always, always, spend less than you earn.

To do this, you can place in each sector the products and services that attract you according to the importance they have in your life, so you will know which ones to postpone and which ones to give priority to.

URGENT AND IMPORTANT	LESS URGENT BUT IMPORTANT
✓ Buy the book I was asked to buy at school.	✓ Buy new shoes to train comfortably.
LESS IMPORTANT BUT URGENT	LESS URGENT AND LESS IMPORTANT
✓ Buy a present for my friend.	✕ Buy snacks to eat on the way home.

47

Donation

Donation is an act of charity, service, generosity, love and empathy that is up to you to do or not to do.

While no one is forcing you to donate, supporting a cause you care about is very good for your personal development.

It is about giving something of yours to a person or a group of people who need it for various reasons.

You can donate toys for deprived children. Cookies for people who do not have enough to eat. Money for research or fights such as the defense of animals or the environment.

In order to donate, you must know what issues and problems in the world make you sensitive and generate the desire to collaborate.

Do you know what cause you would donate something of yours to?

48

Money is limited

I suppose that by now you know that money does not grow from trees, that it is hard to generate, that we must take care of it and that it is a finite good like oil, gold, fresh water or diamonds, and not infinite like air or sunlight.

Therefore, as it ends, you should know very well what to do with it so that it does not run out quickly, or if it does, do not regret what you bought with it, since in most cases you cannot return what you bought and ask for your money back.

I propose that you start labeling your money, separating the daily money for school, the money for your savings and investments, as well as for your leisure and recreation. If you stipulated to spend one dollar per day, stick to the plan.

49

Saving for contingencies

Saving for something you want is all well and good, but it's always important to leave a sum of money set aside just in case.

You may need something or your family may even need a loan from you. That's why it's best to save money for contingencies.

This is something we adults do in case we have an accident, have to solve a problem, or if a loved one needs help.

How much money will you set aside for contingencies?

_____

50

Debts

As I told you a few pages ago, many people generate debt by spending more than they actually have.

It turns out that in the world of adults, banks offer two very appetizing products that we should be wary of.

These are loans and credit cards. For example, if we want to buy a car but we do not have the money to do so, we can resort to a loan from the bank, in which, just as you do when you lend money to a friend, the bank charges interest. But as we are talking about much more money, that value that the bank lends added to the interest it charges for lending is divided into many installments.

At the same time, the bank also grants credit cards, with which you can make purchases without having money at the time and then, once a month you must pay. This can make you lose track of your expenses, since the bank gives you a good amount of money to buy and buy.

You, who are a smart kid and are learning about financial education, will know very well when to take on debt and when not to.

I leave you some questions about it.

If your salary is 1,000 dollars, your fixed expenses (basic needs) are 500 dollars, your savings are 100 dollars and your investments are 100 dollars, how much money do you have left to spend?

If the bank gives you a credit card, what limit will you set yourself to pay each month?

What happens if you can't pay your credit card bill because you exceeded your spending limit?

You will have to stop covering a fixed expense that month, turn to your savings, investments or borrow as a last resort.

51

Retreat

Saving for retirement is a way to guarantee income once you reach the age to stop working.

Now that you are a child you are supported by your parents, when you are an adult you will work yourself, but when you are old you will still have basic needs but neither you nor your parents will be able to support you. Therefore, you will need during your lifetime to guarantee an income for that time.

If you have savings, investments and money set aside for your retirement, you will have peace of mind when you reach old age.

Ask your aunts, uncles, grandparents or elderly neighbors if they saved for their retirement.

52

Budget

To avoid moments of worry or frustration, the best thing to do is to have a budget. There you include all the expenses that are fixed, monthly, basic and that are part of your lifestyle, that is to say, your habits and routine.

In addition, you set aside a sum of money for leisure, entertainment, fun and recreation, and you must use it responsibly and intelligently so that it pays off.

On the other hand, you set aside your money for savings and investments.

This way you will be organized and always have backup money in your pocket.

What percentage of your weekly money goes to entertainment?

53

Invest your savings

You are a child now, and therefore your cash income is not large enough to generate huge sums of savings.

But if you remain consistent and save for a long time, it is likely that your savings will multiply greatly, to the point that it will be more profitable to invest them than to keep saving them.

By that time you will know what to invest them in. But it is important that you manage this information now.

Do you know what stocks are? Do some research about them and leave your answer here.

_____

_____

_____

_____

54

Make your household shopping list

By making a grocery list and shopping under the supervision of accompanying adults, you will be practicing money management skills.

First you go through every cupboard and storage space in the house and write down every item that is missing or will run out soon. Then you review the list with your family for their approval.

Once you have the final list, go to the supermarket with your parents and look for the best prices for those products. It is important that you value quality and above all that you stick to the list and do not go off it.

Propose this to your parents and put it into practice.

55

Exercise patience

Patience is key. Learning not to buy things impulsively is difficult for people of all ages, and even more so for you as a child.

Assuming that if you want something you must wait and save to buy it, is a lesson that can change your life in the future, so trust and handle the frustration or anger of not having everything you want.

What will you buy with your next savings?

How much do you need?

How much have you saved and in what time frame will you be able to complete that amount?

56

Respecting the budget

To avoid falling into temptation and ruining your plan, always buy what you have budgeted for.

This will help you stay focused on your financial goals and you won't be tempted to buy something that caught your eye, but wasn't in your budget.

Remember that if you save you can also acquire what you want, there are no limits to saving and generating money.

How much money do you receive on a weekly basis?

What is your basic weekly fixed cost?

How much do you set aside for savings?

How much do you allocate to investment?

How much money do you have for leisure and fun?

57

Cost and change

When you buy something, you often receive a change. You need to make sure you get the right amount, so you need to exercise.

What are the existing denominations in your currency? Complete the following drawing:

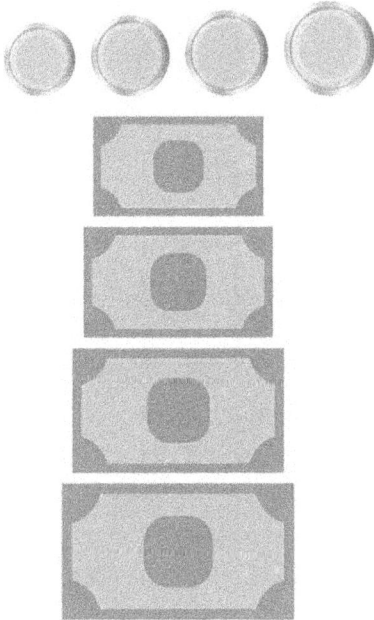

58

Cooking your products

If you haven't started your cookie selling project yet, here is the shopping list and the recipe.

For the cookies you will need:

- 2 eggs
- 250 grams of sugar
- 180 grams of butter
- 1 teaspoon vanilla essence
- 15 grams of baking powder
- 400 grams all-purpose flour
- 200 grams of chocolate chips

The recipe is very simple:

1. In a deep bowl mix the two eggs with the 250 grams of sugar, beat very well with a whisk or fork.
2. Add the 180 grams of butter and the teaspoon of vanilla essence and continue beating.
3. Add to the mixture the 15 grams of baking powder, the 400 grams of all-purpose flour and continue mixing.
4. Finally add the chocolate chips and mix well, this time using a spatula.

5. Let the dough rest in the refrigerator for half an hour. Meanwhile, prepare a buttered and floured baking dish and ask your parents to turn on the oven to 200 degrees.
6. Form 30 small balls with the dough and flatten them on the baking dish, placing them separately from each other as they will grow in the oven.
7. After fifteen minutes of cooking, remove them from the oven and let them cool.

For packaging you can use clear plastic bags and some nice ribbon to close them with a bow.

You can assemble ten packages of three cookies each.

59

Be an energy knight

Saving energy at home is essential for both ecological and economic reasons.

Although a light on may seem normal if you do not have in mind the concept that this action costs money and energy resources, the truth is that the savings you can generate by taking care of this basic service are very important and significant.

You can propose the following to your parents:

Review together the last energy bill and confirm how much energy consumption was that month.

Check the kWh price and if it does not appear, simply divide the total value of the bill by the total kWh consumed.

Propose to your parents that they pay you 50% of the cost of each kWh saved from the next bill, so that the more you help save energy the more your piggy bank is filled.

60

What is the economy?

Economics is a social science that studies the laws governing the production, distribution and consumption of goods and services.

What is production?

_____

_____

_____

_____

What is distribution?

_____

_____

_____

_____

61

Renting: another type of business

Many people choose to buy property instead of keeping their money in the bank, buy shares or start another business, since property hardly loses value, and you can also live on rents.

The key to investing/saving in properties is to rent them. To rent them you make a contract and agree on a monthly payment, which is a sum of money that will increase your monthly income.

Of course, buying a property is not cheap, you must have enough money to do it. For that reason, it will take many years before you recover your invested capital. But it is a safe bet.

Do you and your family live in a rented or owned home?

62

What is inflation?

Inflation and deflation measure the **purchasing power of money**.

Inflation means that prices have increased and therefore with the same income or salary fewer things are bought from one month to the next or from one year to the next.

Deflation means that prices have fallen and, because things are cheaper, more goods and services can be bought with the same money from one month to the next or from one year to the next.

To find out if your country's currency lost or gained value in a monthly or yearly period, for example, you can check how much flour was bought with 10 euros last year and how many kilos of flour are bought with 10 euros today.

Was there inflation or deflation in your country?

123

63

What is a mortgage?

A mortgage loan is a credit granted by the bank, which will be repaid in the medium or long term and must be used for the purchase or improvement of a home.

Since the money for the purchase of the house is granted by the bank, the property belongs to the bank until the person who borrowed the money finishes paying it off.

In case of non-payment, the bank can keep the house and evict its inhabitants.

Do you know someone who bought their home with a mortgage loan?

_____

What is the market value of that house?

_____

How much should you pay the bank?

_____

What are the interests?

64

What does it mean to undertake

To undertake is to take action, to work for it. Whether it is starting a study, a job or a business.

An entrepreneurial person is someone who pursues his goals and objectives, has a plan that he follows steadfastly day by day and is capable of realizing all his dreams.

Entrepreneurship means working on what you start and making it grow.

In relation to financial education, an entrepreneur is someone who works in his own business, does not want to be an employee but aspires to be an entrepreneur.

Invest money (capital) and time (labor) in a business (venture) that will grow into a company.

Would you like to start a business? In what?

65

What are shares?

A share is an ownership purchased over a small fraction of a company, which entitles the investor to a share of the profits.

Thus, with your savings you can buy shares of the company you want, becoming a minority owner of a small fraction of it.

Which company would you like to buy shares of?

66

What are bonds?

A bond is a debt instrument issued by a company or public administration to finance itself.

Whoever needs the financing creates a bond with which he promises to repay the money lent to the buyer of that bond, plus a previously fixed interest rate.

Ask your parents to tell you which bonds are profitable in your country.

67

What is the stock market?

The stock market is a market that is part of the financial system, on which the value assigned to bonds (purchase of debt) and shares (purchase of fractions of a company) depends.

A fall in the place that centralizes the stock market can be a very severe blow to investors.

A wide range of business offerings are interconnected here.

What happened during the stock market crash of 1929?

68

What is impact investing?

Impact investments are those that invest capital in companies with the intention of creating social and environmental benefits beyond financial returns.

Impact investments are investments made in companies and organizations with the intention of generating social and environmental impact.

Name four impactful companies and organizations.

_____

_____

_____

_____

69

The richest person in the world today

In the year 2022, the richest person in the world is Elon Musk, who currently owns 273.5 billion dollars. He is a South African entrepreneur, investor and tycoon who became a naturalized American citizen.

He is the founder, advisor and chief engineer of SpaceX; CEO and product architect of Tesla; founder of The Boring Company; and co-founder of Neuralink and OpenAI.

How old is Elon Musk?

_____

What did Elon Musk study?

_____

What was your first venture?

_____

How did you generate your wealth?

_____

_____

What is Elon Musk investing in now?

_____

What caught your attention about Elon Musk?

_____

_____

_____

_____

70

Contract of receipt of allowance

On this day _____ I agree to receive on a weekly basis the sum of _____ to manage my daily school expenses.

I, _____ am responsible for the administration and use of this money, and **cannot claim or demand an increase** in the amount if I do not arrive on Friday with cash.

Grateful for the opportunity to practice my own financial stewardship, I promise to _____ and _____ that I will use my weekly allowance responsibly.

Signature: _____

71

Contract for domestic services

On the day of _____ I agree to perform _____ times per week the following household chores: _____, _____, _____, _____ with professionalism, dedication and excellence.

The total cost for the service is _____ which I will receive on a weekly basis on _____.

I further agree not to ask for pay in case of failure to perform the tasks correctly.

Grateful for the opportunity to generate my own income, I promise to _____ and _____ that I will use my weekly earnings responsibly.

Signature: _____

72

Savings premium contract

On this day _____ I invite my parents/responsible for
my upbringing _____,
to reward my saving and financial education.

So, for every _____ a week I save, they will donate
_____ to me.

**I agree not to demand this sum that I am given as a
reward in case I do not reach the savings value
stipulated in this contract.**

Signature: _____

73

Contract for use of kitchen

As of today _____ I agree to use the kitchen once a week for cookie making, using my own ingredients financed with my capital and leaving the kitchen in perfect condition, just as I found it.

I will go to an adult to turn on, use and turn off the oven and simply borrow a bowl, fork, spatula and baking dish from the kitchen.

The use of the kitchen for this activity will be on _____ and I will be under the supervision of _____ and/or _____.

Signature: _____

74

Loan agreement

On the day of the date _____, I _____ lend the sum of money _____ to _____ who undertakes to return it on _____ paying the interest of _____.

In case of non-compliance with the stipulated date, an interest of _____ will be charged per day of delay. In addition, if you do not return the full amount within the maximum period of _____ days, I will proceed to appropriate the guarantee you left, which is _____.

Lender's signature: _____

Beneficiary's signature: _____

75

Electricity savings contract

On the day of the date _____, I
_____ pledge to take care of
household electricity consumption, turning off lights in
uninhabited spaces and unplugging appliances that are
not in use.

For each kWh saved, I will be granted 50% of its value on
the bill, which is paid by the adults responsible for my
upbringing, called

_____.

If I have not reduced any kWh on the next bill, I will not be
charged anything and I will assume the risk.

Signature: _____

Beneficiary's signature: _____

76

Benefit coupons

This coupon is good for an ice cream in the park if I have brushed my teeth every day for a week.	This voucher is good for a visit to the amusement park if you have not failed any subject during the entire quarter.
This coupon is good for 50% coverage on a toy of my choice if I have managed to save the remaining 50%.	This coupon is good for a trip to the movies if I have made my bed every day for a consecutive month.

77

Labels for your glass jars

BILLS

INVESTMENT

SAVINGS

78

Final exam

Name four basic necessities that you can buy with money:

_____

_____

_____

_____

Name four basic need services that you can purchase with money:

_____

_____

_____

_____

Name four ways to acquire money:

_____

_____

_____

What is the difference between a wish and a need?

What is the difference between what it costs and what it is worth?

What is the relationship between time and money?

Develop examples of the four things that can be done with money.

Cost savings:

_____

_____

_____

_____

Saving:

_____

_____

_____

_____

Invest:

_____

_____

_____

_____

Donate:

_____

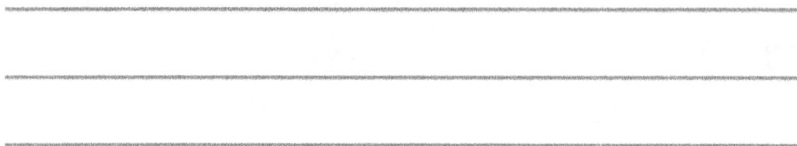

79

Child graduates in basic financial education

Complete the certificate below, cut it out and hang it wherever you like.

Congratulations on making it this far!

You are an enterprising child who will do very well in life because you have knowledge, practice and experience and have learned a lot.

See you next time!

CERTIFICATE

This certificate belongs to:

For his reading, learning, putting into practice and execution of each of the 75 activities for children on financial education that have led him to manage his own money, have savings, investments and be a smart consumer.

Signature of the adult responsible for their upbringing and education

Signature of the applied student

Guide to correct answers

Activity 1: the practices included in financial education are investment, saving, economization, working, entrepreneurship, buying, selling and exchanging.

Activity 2: the tools of financial education are savings, investment, planning and smart spending.

Activity 3: Mischievous sprites are the brands that place products within sight and reach of children in the supermarket so that they bother their parents by asking for them. They are usually expensive and of poor quality.

Activity 5: Products that can be bought with money are, for example, toothpaste, milk, books and bicycles. While services that can be paid with money are electricity, water, wifi and gas.

Activity 9: The basic pillars and needs of a person are, for example, access to housing with services, health, education, food and protection from mistreatment and abuse. The services and goods that one can postpone are going on vacation, going out for lunch, going shopping.

Activity 13: To solve hunger you only need food. To fight boredom the most productive thing to do is to read or go to the park, you don't need to buy anything. If you are thirsty you need to hydrate and for that you need water. If you are sad the best thing to do is to talk to your loved ones and connect with them.

Activity 36: The money cycle is to work, pay bills, make basic purchases, save and invest.

Activity 40: Four examples of buying could be going to the movies, buying ice cream, having internet at home, buying a book. Four examples of selling would be offering a house cleaning service to your parents, selling cookies, selling lemonade, selling fractional candy.

Activity 49: A share is a part of the equity of a publicly traded corporation. Its ownership represents a right of ownership and control of a certain percentage of the company's total. The total number of shares in a company represents the total equity of the company.

Activity 56: Production is the creation of products or services. Distribution is an activity performed to make a product or service available to consumers who want to buy it.

Activity 63: The so-called "Great Depression" originated in the United States from the crash of the New York Stock Exchange on Tuesday, October 29, 1929 and is known as the "Crash of '29" or "Black Tuesday". It was a major global financial crisis.

Activity 64: four impact companies could be Tesla, Amazon, Greenpeace and Toyota.

Activity 75: Four basic necessities are housing, shoes, shelter and food. Four basic services are health, education, water and electricity. Four ways of acquiring money are working, selling something, renting a property, investing. A wish can be postponed for a greater goal, but a need must be able to be fulfilled.

Thank you for choosing my book!

I hope you have learned and enjoyed a lot through this journey and that it helps you create wealth and abundance for you and your loved ones.

If you liked what you read, I would like to have a positive review from you on the page where you got the book. This way you can help me reach out to others and positively impact their lives.

Best wishes!

Christian Lee

www.ingramcontent.com/pod-product-compliance
Lightning Source LLC
Chambersburg PA
CBHW071653210326
41597CB00017B/2197